Jewish Humor
On Your Desktop

By Al Kustanowitz

Volume 5: Yiddish is a Funny Language

Introduction and Acknowledgements

This book is based on some of the funniest of the hundreds of anecdotes that make up my blog, Jewish Humor Central (www.jewishhumorcentral.com).

Six years ago I didn't know what a blog was. My daughter Esther, who has since built a career on blogging and social media, was very patient in explaining to me more than once exactly what she was doing writing one blog, then another, and another. Finally, I got it.

In October 2009, I had an idea. I have always felt that many of my Jewish friends, relatives, and especially professional Jews -- rabbis, cantors, etc. -- take themselves and their observance too seriously. Maybe the seriousness that pervades Jewish religious life in its many forms should be and could be tempered with a touch of humor here and there.

Wouldn't we all be happier and healthier (after all, laughter is the best medicine) if we started each day with a smile, laugh, or even just a grin of recognition at the funny happenings that we, our brethren, and *sistren* experience because of our Jewishness?

That's how the blog called Jewish Humor Central got started. Esther continues to be a strong supporter, and sometimes a source of new material. I also get great satisfaction and support from my sons Jack and Simmy and daughters-in-law Penina and Ilana, who were among the first of my 3,000 plus subscribers in 160 countries.

Finally, Jewish Humor Central would not exist without the loving support of my late wife Shulamit, who edited many of my blog entries and served as a gentle censor of some of the entries that might have otherwise entered the blogosphere with questionable content. This book is dedicated to her memory.

Table of Contents

Cooking in Yiddish

Welcome to the World of Jewish Humor Central

I have been searching for Jewish humor on the Internet ever since the Internet began. You would think that with so many Jewish comedians doing stand-up, TV, and films, there would be an infinite number of web sites with high quality Jewish humor. Well, there aren't. Sure, you'll find some sites with old Jewish jokes, books of Jewish humor included in Amazon's collection, and some hilarious YouTube videos, but you're unlikely to find a single web site that reports regularly on lots of funny things that are happening now in the Jewish world, and also comments on a wide variety of things Jewish that bring a grin, smile, chuckle, laugh, guffaw, or sometimes a sigh to readers.

That's the mission that I undertook for the blog that I named Jewish Humor Central (www.jewishhumorcentral.com). Since starting the blog in October 2009, I have been focusing on Jewish humor in many categories including jokes, stories, parodies, satire, legends, books, films, unbelievable but true happenings, and funny incidents in the news. Some are new, and some are classics. A few are not really funny, but thought provoking. The blog posts include my own comments, but generally rely on the links to tell their own story.

The blog includes items from religious and secular sources of all Jewish denominations, and I strive to keep the site family-friendly. I do not set out to mock or slight any group or subgroup but I can't guarantee that people without a sense of humor will not be offended by some of the posts or links.

So you might ask, "Why a book?" and "Why now?

The nature of a blog is that the many posts (now exceeding 900) appear and disappear quickly. Of course, if you want to take the time to search the archives and keywords on the Jewish Humor Central site, you can find any post going back to the first one. But very few people find the time to do this.

The overnight growth of tablets and smartphones presented an opportunity to organize the best posts by category, present them for display in color and in black-and-white with direct links to the videos and make them available to a wide audience at a very low price.

That's the reason for the book you're reading now, "Jewish Humor on Your Desktop: Vol. 5 – Yiddish is a Funny Language.

This is Volume 5 in a series. The other volumes are also available at Amazon.com. Here are the titles of the books in the series:

Jewish Humor on Your Desktop

If you have the interactive eBook edition, just click on each URL to link directly to the video clips. In this print editon we provide the URLs; you will have to type them into your internet browser bar to see the videos.

I hope that Jewish Humor on Your Desktop brings joy and laughter into your home, on your desktop PC or Mac, and wherever you carry your laptop, tablet, and smartphone – not just on Purim, but throughout the year.

Enjoy!

Al Kustanowitz
Blogger-in-Chief

Yiddish is a Funny Language

Yiddish, the mamme-loshn (mother tongue) of the Jews of Eastern Europe for centuries, has had its ups and downs. It has been spoken and written by Chassidic Jews who still use it today as their vernacular language while they treat Hebrew as a holy language not suited for everyday common speech. It has a long history as the basis of a rich secular Jewish culture that included books, magazines, plays, and films.

And, we may add, jokes. Most of the comedians of the early to mid-20th century grew up listening to jokes and funny songs and stories from the Yiddish theater, which strongly influenced their development of American humor with a Yiddish inflection.

This book presents anecdotes and associated video clips that illustrate the colorful humor associated with the Yiddish language. Whether it's Yiddish jokes, Yiddish words and expressions, Yiddish song and dance, Yiddish in theater and film, or Yiddish cooking, you will chuckle at the ways this language of an Eastern Europe that was thought to be long gone has permeated modern Jewish life around the world today.

Yiddish Humor and Comedy

Herschel Fox Shares Funny Israeli Personal Want Ads

Fluent in Yiddish and Hebrew, Herschel Fox has appeared in countless night clubs, theatres and synagogues throughout the United States. He has shared the stage with artists such as Jan Peerce, Mickey Katz, and Molly Picon.

Primarily a cantor, having trained with Cantor David Koussevitzky and Sidor Belarsky, he has held positions in synagogues in Connecticut, New York, and California. Together with his wife Judy, who is the cantor in the Synagogue for the Performing Arts in Los Angeles (where Joseph Telushkin is the rabbi), they perform as the Fox Cantors.

But Herschel is also a stand-up comedian and loves to tell stories in Yinglish. Here is a video of his performance for the International Association of Yiddish Clubs (yes, there are 94 of them around the world).

In this video, Herschel shares his collection of funny Israeli personal want ads with the enthusiastic audience. Following the comedy video, we include a short sample of the Fox Cantors singing.

Type the URLs in your browser address bar to see the videos: http://youtu.be/Uwcxu0vENTk http://youtu.be/NT1ViGvvim4

Eleanor Reissa: Yiddish Comedy in Music - Be Happy...But Not Too Happy

Eleanor Reissa has sung all over the world in solo shows, with bands and orchestras, in English and in Yiddish, in small private venues and in thousand seat theatres.

Her solo show, *Hip, Heymish, and Hot*, garnered rave reviews off-Broadway and in Florida's Parker Playhouse.

Besides singing solo, she has sung with Theo Bikel, Mike Burstyn, Bruce Adler, Claire Barry, Neil Sedaka, the Klezmer Conservatory Band, Frank London and the Klezmatics and many many others.

In October 2010, Reissa performed in concert at the Museum of Jewish Heritage in downtown New York. In this video clip, she sings the Yiddish song Freylakh Zayn (Be Happy). But in a comedic introduction to the song for non-Yiddish speakers, she launches into a description of Jewish life in Brooklyn and why it's OK to be happy, but not too happy.

Type the URL in your browser address bar to see the video: http://youtu.be/VVvwH8j8kLQ

Chassidic Comedy with Menashe Lustig: Pesach Car Wash Commercial

We've been running a series of funny commercials from Israel ever since we started Jewish Humor Central, (You can see them all in Volume 2 of this series, "Israel is a Funny Country") but we found that the Chassidic community in Brooklyn can also be a good source of funny ads and slapstick comedy.

Menashe Lustig, who calls himself Mr. Chusid, appears in a series of comedy sketches. Most of the dialogue is in Yiddish, but the comedy is broad and expressive and can be understood without mastering the *mama loshen.*

Just in time for Pesach, Lustig, after burning his chometz and reciting the appropriate blessing, proceeds to look for chometz in his car and clean it. Frustrated with the mess and dirty appearance of the car, he first tries to use his yarmulke as a rag to wash the trunk lid, and then gives up. He calls his wife to get the number of a car wash that sponsors the skit, asking her to spell out the number in Yiddish (347-WASH) by repeating "W as in Velvel, A as in Anything, S as in Shin and H as in Hock Nisht Keyn Tchainik."

We hope you'll enjoy this when the time comes to clean for Passover.

Type the URL in your browser address bar to see the video: http://youtu.be/Puy3DuHk9HY

More Chassidic Comedy with Menashe Lustig: The Unspoken Language

How far can the expression "nu" and a few grunts and sighs get you in a lively telephone conversation? If you're Chassidic comedian Menashe Lustig, it can get you pretty far.

We shared some of Lustig's Pesach shtick with you (see above) -- a funny ad for a car wash. Now he's at it again, with a two and a half minute phone session with an unseen caller. Not a real word is spoken, just "nu" over and over again, combined with a collection of hand motions and body language.

A Sqverer Chassid from New Square in New York's Rockland County, Lustig has his own Facebook page, but you'll have to know Hebrew and Yiddish to read all of the entries there.

Type the URL in your browser address bar to see the video: http://youtu.be/vc90wQiFe1E

Nachas, Mensch, Nudnik, and 60 More: Jewish Pride Expressed In Vanity License Plates

As you drive on the highway or pass parked cars, do you ever notice license plates with Jewish, Hebrew, or Yiddish words and themes? Don't we all, at one time or another?

Well, some people make a hobby of it. Melanie Rubin of San Diego, California, has accumulated a collection of photos of plates that make a decidedly Jewish statement.

Rubin, a writer for the San Diego Jewish World, works at the Jewish Community Center and participates in Jewish events at other venues throughout San Diego County. That makes her well-positioned to spot and photograph Jewish-themed license plates wherever she goes.

The San Diego Jewish World maintains the photo collection on their web site where you can see all 63 plates. Misha Marmar, a Russian singer of Yiddish songs, has recorded a video, singing *Vi bist du gevein* to accompany a slide presentation of many of these license plates.

Type the URL in your browser address bar to see the video: http://youtu.be/QRyVMr9fKw8

Classic Jokes Translated From Yiddish on Jewish Heritage Tour

There's nothing like an old Jewish joke told in Yiddish by a veteran Yiddish speaker for whom these jokes are part of his vocabulary. Such storytellers in the original Yiddish are getting harder and harder to find. Interest in old Jewish jokes told by old Jews has grown in the last few years, as we have seen with the popularity of the website Old Jews Telling Jokes and the recent publication of many of these jokes in book form.

In 2007, a Jewish Heritage tour of Ukraine featured Klezmer musicians and other entertainment while cruising along the Dnieper river. The participants in the cruise, called Dnieper Shleppers, were treated to a virtuoso stream of Yiddish joke telling by Abe Bartel, an elderly Yiddish speaker from Paris. The audience howled with laughter as the jokes, some of them off-color, were translated in deadpan style by Professor Eugene Orenstein of McGill University. Here is a video of the joke session. Listen carefully and enjoy!

Type the URL in your browser address bar to see the video: http://youtu.be/I_2ZTykIrxo

Mentsch or Shmuck? Michael Wex Tells How To Be and How Not To Be

There are people out there, millions of them, who act as if they still believe everything that their mothers told them in the first six months of their life: they're the nicest, most beautiful, most promising and intelligent bags of flesh ever to walk the earth, and anybody who can't see it is a jealous fool.

We call these people *shmucks*. In his new book, *How to Be a Mentsh (and Not a Shmuck)*, published by Harper Collins, bestselling author Michael Wex (*Born to Kvetch* and *Just Say Nu*) offers a wise and witty guide to being a good human being (*A mentsh*) regardless of your religion or beliefs—a blueprint for living a decent and moral life, acting with self-control instead of self-denial, and winning through cooperation rather than competition.

But this is no dull manual about loving thy neighbor. It's a fast-paced and entertaining adventure in the wisdom of the ages, wherever that wisdom may be found: Yiddish proverbs, current events, Talmudic stories, movies, television, and more. Referencing pop culture and Jewish tradition with equal ease, Wex explores the strategies developed by an oppressed people to pursue happiness with their dignity—and sense of humor—intact.

You can get the flavor of the book by reading a few pages from the publisher's website. It's a very readable combination of humor, etymology, pop culture, and Jewish history.

Here's an interview with the author on WatchMojo.com, where he talks about the art of mentshlichkeit and how to avoid being a shmuck.

Type the URL in your browser address bar to see the video: http://youtu.be/k-B7JzmGLKA

Yiddishology 101

How Good Is Your Yiddish? "Shtipper or Shtupper"

The Tampa Jewish Community Center and Federation has been testing the Yiddish vocabulary of its members on a weekly basis by videotaping "person in the street" interviews, similar to the "Jaywalking" sketches that Jay Leno has been doing for years and the "Jew Walking" video that we included in Volume 3 of this series (Humor in Jewish Life).

Random members of the community are asked the meaning of a common, usually funny sounding, Yiddish word, and their spontaneous reactions are videotaped for us to enjoy.

Our first Yiddishology sketch tries to uncover the meaning of *shtipper*, also pronounced *shtupper*.

Watch, laugh, and enjoy.

Type the URL in your browser address bar to see the video: http://youtu.be/wjWINJSoQ4Q

How Good Is Your Yiddish? "Kenahora (Kanahora)"

It's back to Tampa to watch community center members trying to uncover the meaning of *kenahora*, also spelled *kanahora* or *kinahora*. Which definition do you think is correct?

Type the URL in your browser address bar to see the video: http://youtu.be/oHW2WqE_cHs

How Good Is Your Yiddish?
"Ungapatchka/Ungepatchket"

Can you explain the meaning of the Yiddish verb *ungapatchka*, also pronounced *ungepatchke*. (The adjective is *ungepatchket*.)

Let's see how the experts in Tampa do. In the meantime, try to think of someone or something that's really *ungepatchket*!

Type the URL in your browser address bar to see the video: http://youtu.be/E2U-EKnr0V8

How Good Is Your Yiddish? "Shlimazel"

The best example we've heard of a *shlimazel* (probably an amalgam of *shlecht mazel* or bad luck) and its differentiation from a *shlemiel* is that the *shlemiel* is the one who spills the soup, and the *shlimazel* (or *shlemazel*) is the one who has the soup spilled on him.

Type the URL in your browser address bar to see the video: http://youtu.be/vwlLQeOVyRE

How Good Is Your Yiddish? "Shmegegge"

We weren't entirely satisfied with the final definition in the video clip below, so we did some independent research. Remember our explanation (see above) that the *shlimazel* is the one that the *shlemiel* spills soup on? Well, it turns out that the *shmegegge* is the one who cleans up the soup that was spilled on the *shlimazel* by the *shlemiel*. Who knew?

Type the URL in your browser address bar to see the video: http://youtu.be/helvj8W7w2o

How Good Is Your Yiddish? "Tchotchke"

We have some *tchotchkes* around the house, mostly from trade shows, conventions, conferences, and seminars spanning four decades. The word has made it into the Merriam-Webster Dictionary and many other online dictionaries. Let's see how the Floridians react in the man-in-the-street interviews in this video. How many *tchotchkes* do you have in your house?   Maybe it's time to get rid of them.

P. S. Don't confuse *tchotchke* with *tsatskele*. Although the words come from the same root, their usage conveys entirely different meanings. *Tchotchke* usually means a worthless trinket or souvenir. A *tsatskele* is usually a young woman or teenage girl who is a handful, very demanding, or "a piece of work." But it can also mean bimbo or dear little child. It all depends on inflection, how the word is expressed. Go figure!

Type the URL in your browser address bar to see the video: http://youtu.be/L4mijk5KAg4

How Good Is Your Yiddish? "Halevai"

It's back to the Tampa Jewish Community and their person-in-the street interviews to test for knowledge of Yiddish expressions. Now it's time to see how many know the meaning of *halevai*.

Strictly speaking, *Halevai* is a Hebrew word that, along with many others, found its way into the Yiddish language. Of course we know it means "if only" or "it should only be so". Let's see how close the Tampanese come.

Type the URL in your browser address bar to see the video: http://youtu.be/oG0FtKmm4bk

Halevai is the title of a song composed by Moishe Oysher and recorded by him and The Barry Sisters in the 1950s.

Type the URL in your browser address bar to see the video: http://youtu.be/1JYJAaeHwIo

How Good Is Your Yiddish? "Balabusta"

After asking a range of people to define *balabusta (the actual pronunciation is closer to balabuste)*, the off-camera man-in-the-street silent interviewer asks Yiddish expert and author Michael Wex to deliver the final word, leaving no doubt as to its meaning.

We thought we'd add a little etymology, explaining the word's origin.

In Hebrew, the master of the house is literally the *ba'al ha'bayit, or ba'al ha'bayis*. The words, when they transmuted into Yiddish, became balabus. It's fairly common in Yiddish for a male term, when converted to its female equivalent, to take on the ending *"te"* or *"ene,"* e.g. chazzan-chazzante, yid-yidene. Thus for every *balabus* there is usually a *balabuste*. This is one word that is almost always positive, expressing admiration for a woman who can take hold of a home and manage it well.

Type the URL in your browser address bar to see the video: http://youtu.be/8TyFC9KGIA0

How Good Is Your Yiddish? "Plotz"

It's one last trip to Tampa, where the Yiddishologists at the Tampa Jewish Community Center are out in full force once again, this time trying to zero in on the best definition of the Yiddish word *plotz*.

The Tampanese so far have volunteered definitions of *shtupper, kenahora, ungapatchka, shlimazel*, and *shmegegge, tchotchke, halevai, and balabusta*. Some of the clips are so funny, we could *plotz* from laughter. So thanks again, Tampa, for giving us some language lessons along with lots of fun.

Type the URL in your browser address bar to see the video: http://youtu.be/kVW6wsr3keI

Yiddish And Danish: A New Funny Video Dictionary From Shtetl Montreal

Shtetl, a new online alternative Jewish magazine from Montreal, has started a series of short video clips of Yiddish speakers enunciating and explaining some familiar Yiddish words and expressions. Some are straightforward and (WARNING!) some are a bit salty.

What do you expect? Yiddish is not a holy and pure language, but one which has embodied the triumphs and tragedies of Eastern European Jews for the last few centuries. Over time, it has picked up expressions reflecting a knowledge of and respect for Jewish religious tradition as well as street wisdom acquired from everyday living.

To get things started, we're sharing three expressions that kick off the series. When the dictionary was started in 2011, we were looking forward to a full list of definitions. But they only posted eight, and we have them all here.

Oh, if you're wondering how the language of Denmark fits into the picture, it doesn't. Danish refers to the pastries served to the speakers as they record their comments.

Type the URLs in your browser address bar to see the videos:

A chazer blaybt a chazer: http://youtu.be/9LevGSYwWfM

Az di bubbe volt gehat beytsim...:
http://youtu.be/0Fzwf9DR3Sc

Feh!: http://youtu.be/FeioaBNYB5U

Vos machst du?: http://youtu.be/ekWQkEKYIQU

Bulvan: http://youtu.be/CUsr4DZCykM

Brocha: http://youtu.be/VwPiXN_mBm0

A chalerya: http://youtu.be/a4av2_fhG4s

Du host a langer tsung: http://youtu.be/wRkYDunEack

Hock mir nisht kein chainik: http://youtu.be/ZZVSMT-y3bc

Zol er lebn...ober nit lang: http://youtu.be/Sx0V6wqwfTI

Chutzpah: http://youtu.be/rcbQXfgKvTg

Gefilte Fish: http://youtu.be/fCImDPrTC64

Yiddish Book Center Students Choose Their Favorite Yiddish Words

The National Yiddish Book Center, founded by Aaron Lansky in 1980 to rescue Yiddish books, has been offering a summer program in recent years. The Steiner Summer Program at the Center, in Amherst, Massachusetts, offers 18 qualified full-time college students an intensive educational experience in Yiddish language, literature, culture, and history.

The graduates of the 2010 summer session were asked to pick their favorite Yiddish word. In this video, the students hem and haw their way through making their selections, but finally declare their favorites, in most cases (but not all) pronouncing them correctly.

Some of the choices are based on meaning, some on the sound, and some because just saying it gives them a special feeling.

Type the URL in your browser address bar to see the video: http://www.yiddishbookcenter.org/video/favorite-yiddish-words

The story of the founding of the center is interesting in its own right, and the following video shows how it got started: http://youtu.be/Hilw6zj-XD8

Close Encounters with the Yiddish Language

New York Times Gives Journalist A Pain In Tuches

In June 2010, Jeffrey Goldberg, national correspondent of The Atlantic magazine, was interviewed by Helene Cooper of the New York Times as part of a story she wrote in the Week in Review section.

Here is the quote:

"I don't necessarily believe you solve all of America's problems in Iraq, Afghanistan, Pakistan and Yemen by freezing settlement growth. On the other hand, there's no particular reason for Israel to make itself a pain in the tush either."

But Goldberg didn't say "*tush*." He said "*tuches*." (also spelled *tuchis* and *tukhis*). And therein lays the predicament. It seems the Times has a problem with printing Yiddish words that, while not exactly dirty, could offend some of its readers. Witness the angst another Times writer experienced earlier this month when wrestling with how and how many times the "newspaper of record" would permit him to use the title of an upcoming movie, "Dinner for Schmucks."

A few days later, Goldberg explained the censorship to readers of his Atlantic blog this way:

When Helene first interviewed me, I actually used the word "*tuchus*," rather than "*tush*," but she phoned back a couple of hours later to tell me that the newspaper's Special Committee for the Proper Deployment of Yiddishisms ruled that "*tuchus*" is insufficiently elegant, and so could I please offer a substitute. I asked Helene for a suggestion, and she came up with "*tushie*." I responded by questioning whether the word "*tushie*" could be considered more elegant than the word "*tuchus*." I also told her that I could not allow myself to be quoted using the word "*tushie*" because I am no longer four years old.

But because I am prone to compromise (witness my position on the issue of the two-state solution, as well as on the theoretical idea of sharing Jerusalem), I agreed to substitute "*tush*" for "*tuchus*," which I came to regret when Helene's colleague, and our mutual friend, Mark Leibovich, used a non-Yiddish vulgarity, namely, "pussy," by way of denouncing me for my use of the word "*tush*" in a sentence.

Commenting on this verbal contretemps, Philologos, the erudite language columnist at the Jewish Daily Forward, offers what would seem to be the definitive explanation of the word in question and its origins:

One may be permitted to doubt whether the Times actually has a Committee for the Proper Deployment of Yiddishisms (although if anyone did have one, it *would* be the Times), but otherwise, Goldberg's account rings true. Which leads one to ask: How "inelegant" would "tuchus" have been? Is this Yiddish word really, as the editors of the Times think, the semantic and connotative equivalent of the English word "ass," which the Times deems too vulgar to print?

Michael Wex, the highly knowledgeable and always entertaining author of three books on Yiddish usage, seems to think that it is. In his "Just Say Nu," Wex, who doesn't have a censorial bone in his body, has a boxed section titled "A Bar Mitzvah of Behinds," in which he presents us with "Thirteen [Yiddish] designations for the human rear (in declining order of politeness.)" These are, with Wex's English translations and transliterations (which follow the Polish rather than the more standard Lithuanian pronunciation of Yiddish): 1) *Hintn,* rear; 2) *Hinterkhaylek,* hindpart; 3) *Interkhaylek,* underpart; 4) *Gezess,* seat, buttocks; 5) *Zitser,* sitter, seat; 6) *Zitsflaysh,* seat-meat. 7) *Di mekheeleh,* The I-beg-your-pardon; 8) *Der Vee-hayst-men-es,* The whatchamacallit. 9) *Der vee-dee-yeedn-hobm-gereet;* The where-the-Jews-rested. 10) *Ookher,* rear, behind; 11) *Akhoreiyim,* hindparts; 12) *Morsh,* ass; 13) *Tukhes,* ass.

This is followed by a page of commentary, in which, among other things, Wex points out that Expression 9, *Vu-di-yidn-hobn-gerut* (to use standard Yiddish transliteration), is a witty allusion to the Bible. There, in Chapter 33 of the Book of Numbers, in an account of the Children of Israel's wanderings in the desert, we find the verse, "And they departed from Makhelot and encamped at Tahat." The place-name Tahat, which occurs nowhere else in Scripture, is spelled and pronounced the same as the Hebrew word *taḥat,* which means both "under" and, in modern Hebrew, the rear end. It is from *taḥat* that Yiddish gets *tukhis,* and from *tukhis* that American Jewish English gets "tush" and "tushie."

What more can we add, other than we've observed the use of the word in business situations, as in "tuches af'n tish," (literally "rear end on the table") meaning "put up or shut up" or "let's get down to brass tacks."

Our conclusion? The New York Times is definitely Yiddishly-challenged. Since they appoint special editors like the Public Editor (ombudsman) to comment on journalistic issues, we'd like to suggest that they hire Philologos or Michael Wex (or if they're busy, Jewish Humor Central) to clue them in on the true meanings of any Yiddish words their writers slip into their columns.

Yiddish is Alive and Well in the 21st Century

What Grows on a Yiddish Farm? Yiddish Speakers, of Course

Did you ever wonder what it would be like to go back to nature and work on a farm for the summer while speaking only Yiddish? A group of ten eager participants are doing just that this summer in a farming community located in Goshen, New York, just an hour north of New York City.

Founded by Yisroel Bass and Naftali Ejdelman and funded by grants from Jewish foundations, the Yiddish Farm was established as a venue for Yiddish language immersion and Yiddish programs, ranging in length from a weekend to three months. It functions as a real organic farm, raising vegetables for sale in nearby towns.

In 1939, over 75% of Jews spoke Yiddish as their primary language. There were over 150 daily newspapers worldwide, and at least 12 Yiddish theaters in New York alone. Tragically, the language has been passed down to only a fraction of today's youth, though more than 50% of American Jews descend from Yiddish-speakers.

In recent years there has been a Yiddish revival, with the language now being taught in over 50 universities throughout the world. The Klezmer revival has popularized Jewish folk music across continents, and over 10,000

Yiddish books are now available on the internet free of charge.

Workers on the farm and attendees at its programs are now getting the opportunity to speak Yiddish outside of the classroom and restore it to a living language.

Get a close-up view of how these goals are being met in this video of life on the Yiddish Farm.

Type the URL in your browser address bar to see the video: http://vimeo.com/45978742

KlezKamp, Yiddish Brigadoon, Comes To Life In Catskills

If you're a fan of the American musical theatre, you'll remember the 1947 Broadway show *Brigadoon*, the story of a mysterious Scottish village that appears for only one day every hundred years, though to the villagers, the passing of each century seems no longer than one night.

Well, there's a Jewish version. Every year, in the last week of December, hundreds of people gather in what used to be the Granit Hotel in Kerhonkson, in New York's Catskill Mountains, to immerse themselves in Yiddish culture -- song, dance, language, but most important - klezmer.

Joseph Berger wrote an article about KlezKamp in The New York Times Arts section in November 2010. Here is an excerpt:

Not only were the evening music and dance programs a tribute to vigorous life, but those who took part in the courses — more than 50 were offered, with six sessions apiece — also seemed to revel in the chance to reacquaint themselves with the unmatched expressions they had heard from their bubbes (grandmothers) and zaydes (grandfathers) and the dance steps they had not done since a cousin's bar mitzvah long ago.

Words tossed about during the week included not just those like kvetch and kibitz, which have entered American idiom, but also fresher candidates like shreklekh (terrible or frightening), naches (prideful joy), farblondget (mixed up) and luftmensch (an impractical person with no apparent income).

Henry Sapoznik, a Ukrainian cantor's son who helped found KlezKamp in 1984, calls it a "Yiddish Brigadoon," a gathering, like the Scottish village in that 1947 musical, that comes to life once in a long while after a lengthy snooze. His co-founder, Adrienne Cooper, calls it "a flying shtetl." But both say that over 25 years the thousands who have taken part have knitted together into a group that stays in touch year round.

Type the URL in your browser address bar to see the video: http://youtu.be/w0kLAw43KWU

Yiddish Song and Dance

Di Mamme Iz Gegangen - Delightful Animation of a Classic Yiddish Song

"Almonds and Wine" brings a Yiddish folk song to life, as the animated journey of a young bride and groom from Eastern Europe to North America is set to rollicking klezmer music.

Fleeing the threat of war, the couple arrives in Canada, establish a new life together and hand down their traditions to the generations that follow. This film is set to a classic Yiddish folk song, *Di Mamme iz Gegangen in Mark Arayn* (My Mother Went to Market.) It was produced, directed and animated by Arnie Lipsey.

The animation is inspired, but the characters move through the story so fast that you'll have to watch it more than once or keep your finger on the pause button to catch all of the details and read what's written on the store signs and protest signs.

How do we know that the couple settles in Canada and not the U.S.? Notice that the boy is running around with a hockey stick, not a baseball bat.

The depiction of the Jewish wedding ceremony is very detailed. Be sure to watch for the expression on the bride's and groom's faces when they are lifted onto chairs for the traditional handkerchief dance.

Type the URL in your browser address bar to see the video: http://youtu.be/RKiooqeMBJc

Here are the Yiddish lyrics and English translation:

Oy di mamme iz gegangen in mark arayn noch keyln,
Oy hot zi mir tzurik gebracht a meydele fun Peyln.
Oy iz dos a meydele a sheyns un a feyns,
Oy Mit di shvartse eygelach, oy ketsele du mayns.

Oy di mamme iz gegangen in mark arayn noch kreyt,
Oy hot zi mir tzurik gebracht a meydele fun beyt,
Oy iz dos a meydele a sheyns un a feyns,
Oy mit di shvartse eygelach, oy ketsele du mayns.

Oy di mamme is gegangen in mark noch a katchke
Oy hot zi mir tzurik gebracht a meydele, a tzatzke
Oy iz dos a meydele a sheyns un a feyns,
Oy mit di vayse tzeyndelach, oy ketsele du mayns.

Ich hob gegesn mandlen, ich hob getrunken vayn,
Ich hob gelibt a meydele un ken on ir nisht zayn,
Oy iz dos a meydele a sheyns un a feyns,
Oy mit di roite bekelach, oy ketsele du mayns.

My mother went to market to buy some coal,
She brought me back a lovely girl from Poland.

Oh what a girl she was, how beautiful and fine,
Ah, those black eyes of hers, ah, you kitten of mine.

My mother went to market to buy some cabbage,
She brought me back a girl just off a coach.
Oh what a girl she was, how beautiful and fine,
Ah, those black eyes of hers, ah, you kitten of mine.

My mother went to market to buy a duck,
She brought me back a girl - what a handful!
Oh what a girl she was, how beautiful and fine,
Ah, those white teeth of hers, ah, you kitten of mine.

I have been eating almonds, I have been drinking wine,
And I have loved a lass and could not part from her.
O what a lass she was, how lovely and how fine,
Ah, those red cheeks of hers, ah, you kitten of mine.

Netherlands Klezmer Group Plays and Sings "Der Rebbe Elimelech"

The band *Die Drei Dudelim* ('the three players of tunes') consists of three good friends who have been playing Klezmer music since 1994. Their music is heavily inspired by the old Eastern European Klezmer tradition, but with a modern 'feel', and it clearly reveals their classical music education. The Dudelim are multi-instrumentalists, playing several guitars, violin, clarinet, and mandolin as well as double bass, but they also distinguish themselves by their excellent vocals. The moods of their songs vary from quiet and melancholic to vibrant, fast, and full of excitement.

In this video they play a Yiddish classic, *Der Rebbe Elimelech*, sort of a Yiddish version of Old King Cole. Just in case you don't know this Yiddish standard, it describes an Eastern European rabbi who has a little too much to drink when Shabbat ends and becomes more and more happy and boisterous as the evening progresses.

First he takes off his tefillin and puts on his glasses, and calls for two fiddlers. Then he makes Havdalah, calls for the shamash and two cymbal players. Finally he takes off his hat and puts on his kittel and calls for two drummers. The music reaches a crescendo when the fiddlers drum, the drummers play the cymbals, and the cymbal players fiddle (or some such combination -- you get the idea.)

Type the URL in your browser address bar to see the video: http://youtu.be/v3wA89enABg

Israeli Singer Moti Giladi Performs Sinatra's "My Way" His Way - In Yiddish

We always find it enjoyable to watch Yiddish translations of popular music, whether pop songs or Gilbert and Sullivan operas. We're particularly fond of the Yiddish versions of The Mikado and The Pirates of Penzance.

So when we saw a new YouTube posting of a Yiddish version of Frank Sinatra's *My Way,* we thought of sharing it with you. This version was sung by Israeli singer Moti Giladi at a Jewish Music Festival in Warsaw in 2007.

Singing to a full house in a large auditorium, Giladi gives a strong performance of the classic ballad in Yiddish translation. So how do you translate the title? At first hearing, we thought it was "My Vei." But after a few replays, we're pretty sure it's "Mein Veg." Enjoy!

http://youtu.be/ri_YVKgc3e0

Looking For Yiddish Cabaret? How About Di Goldene Pave At The Blue Note Club In Milan?

OK, we know, it's a long way to go to see five women in glittering gold gowns singing Yiddish songs, playing piano, violin, and cello. But where else but a jazz club in Milan, Italy can you see such an ensemble in action? And the music, the music! Tumbalalaika, Dona Dona, Der Neier Sher, and Yiddish wedding music.

The performers call their act *Di Goldene Pave* (pronounced pav-eh) - In Yiddish, The Golden Peacock. The act recently premiered at the Blue Note cabaret/jazz club in Milan. This group consists of five professional musicians/singers coming from different European countries. The quintet does vocals, light percussion, violin, viola, cello, piano as well as backing vocalists, playing all the different flavors of Jewish music, from Klezmer to Yiddish songs to Spanish/Sephardi music, to Yemenite folk song.

The *Goldene Pave* are:

Angelica Dettori: vocals and light percussions
Luviona Hasani: violin and backing voice
Eriola Gripshi: viola and backing voice
Cecilia Salmé: cello and backing voice
Valentina Verna: piano and backing voice

And you really don't have to travel to Italy to see them. Here are a few of their videos for your enjoyment: *Tumbalalaika, Dona Dona*, and *Tanz Tanz Yiddelach*.

Type the URLs in the browser address bar to see the videos: http://youtu.be/PapAvrnyVZg
http://youtu.be/a2nbqxA8Jec
http://youtu.be/JvsOMQt4GT8

Yidden, Popular Yiddish Wedding Song and Dance, Was Originally a German Song About Genghis Khan's Conquests and Sexual Prowess

One of the most frequently played songs at Jewish weddings for the last few decades has been *Yidden Yidden, Kumt Aheim,* the fervent dance introduced by Mordechai Werdyger (professionally known as Mordechai Ben David, or MBD) in 1986.

Everybody assumes that it's a Jewish song. But like Hatikva (adapted from an Italian madrigal) and some other popular Jewish songs, it has its origins in a country and culture that is in no way Jewish.

The reality is that the music that we recognize as *Yidden* first appeared at the Eurovision song competition in 1979, the year that saw Israel win first place for the song *Hallelujah* by the group called Milk and Honey.

That year, Germany entered the competition with a song praising the strength and sexual prowess of Genghis Khan, the 13th century Mongol conqueror. The song is titled *Dschinghis Khan*, by a band of the same name.

Here are some of the translated lyrics:

He was the greatest lover and the strongest man of his day
And we have heard that all the women fell for him, so they say.

And he bred seven children in one long night
He had his girls around him in his very sight
And nothing that could stop him in this world.
Geng-Geng-Genghis Khan, etc.

Here's the video, sung in 1979 in the original German, with English subtitles:

http://youtu.be/7i9ozy739c8

Here's the same song, now in Yiddish, sung at a Chabad telethon ten years later by MBD, often referred to in Orthodox and Chassidic circles as the King of Jewish Music:
http://youtu.be/FVwGKo2pOmc

Celebrating Classic Jewish Music Then, Now, and Forever: Chiribim

Music has always been an important part of Jewish life, and it has thrived in the shetel in Europe, on the Lower East Side of New York, the Yiddish theater, on Broadway, in concert halls worldwide, and in schools, Jewish and non-Jewish, everywhere.

Some of the classic melodies, once thought to be headed for extinction, have experienced a revival. One of the most popular, Chiribim Chiribom, has been showing up in performances around the world in recent days. The song was first recorded by Moishe Oysher in 1931 and became popular in the late 1950s when the Barry Sisters recorded a lively, schmaltzy version.

The videos below show the wide range of interpretation of this classic melody. Type the URLs in the browser address bar to see the videos.

First, the Guilboa dance troupe performing in Cartagena, Spain. http://youtu.be/FeYER-qd5t8

Next, a performance by Efim Aleksandrov in Moscow. As Kim Murphy wrote in the Los Angeles Times,

The distance Russia has traveled since the Communist years, with their official bans on public worship and discrimination in jobs and education — the latter hardship facilitated by the hated designation of Jews' ethnicity on Soviet internal passports — was apparent last month, when Jewish pop artist Efim Alexandrov-Zitzerman sang a concert of Yiddish songs to a sold-out hall in the prestigious Rossiya Hotel, in the shadow of the Kremlin.

"We are the link whose mission is to reconnect the broken tradition. The songs of our grandmothers and grandfathers must be heard by our children, and then by the children of our children," Alexandrov-Zitzerman told a hall of emotional concertgoers.

http://youtu.be/artkqUuVvRo

We could include many more performances, but we'll end this post with Barbarella Halliwell and Editta Chal Bacio reinterpreting the Barry Sisters' act. Enjoy!

http://youtu.be/795xg6AbLvU

Mike Burstyn Sings Hu Tza Tza at Chabad Telethon

Every year we wait for the night of fun, music, and good feelings that come with the annual Chabad Telethon. A big fundraiser for the worldwide organization, it always features top names in the entertainment field, both Jewish and non-Jewish.

And what Jewish show would be complete without a star turn by Mike Burstyn? In this clip he shows his Second Avenue heritage with a comic routine, during which (if you count carefully) he rattles off eight old jokes while singing a classic Yiddish vaudeville tune, *Hu Tza Tza.*

Type the URL in your browser address bar to see the video: http://youtu.be/hM-RPd27qhc

More Than a Hora: Israeli Teenage Ballroom Dance Champs Perform to Hebrew and Yiddish Medley

If you thought Israeli dancing meant doing the hora or a mitzvah tantz, it's time to update your knowledge of Israel and what Israelis are doing at home and on the world scene.

Teen Dancers Michael Lerner and Marika Odikadze recently won the Israeli Junior Championship in Ballroom Dancing in the 16 to 18 age group, and represented Israel in international competitions sponsored by the International DanceSport Federation in Linz, Austria.

We caught a glimpse of Michael and Marika dancing to a medley of familiar Hebrew and Yiddish songs, including *Hava Nagila, L'Chayim, Papirossen, Chiribim, Bublichki, Tumbalalaika, Where Do I Begin (Love Story), Cabaret*, and *Hevenu Shalom Aleichem*, as sung by The Barry Sisters and other singers.

Type the URL in your browser address bar to see the video: http://youtu.be/2bbZcoGl6io

Yiddish in Theater and Film

"Di Yam Gazlonim": The Pirates of Penzance in Yiddish

Can you picture a performance of Gilbert and Sullivan's *The Pirates of Penzance* -- in Yiddish? You may see it -- and many other musicals and plays, if negotiations now underway in the world of Yiddish theater are successful.

The Folksbiene troupe (formerly called the National Yiddish Theater-Folksbiene) has been a presence on the Jewish theater scene for 95 years. It's the last survivor of the dozen or more theaters that thrived on the Lower East Side in the early 1900's, but two years ago it found that a new theater group, the New Yiddish Repertory Company had arrived and started a sort of competition for the same small audience.

Yiddish theater lovers, concerned about its future, are trying to bring the two groups together and collaborate, if not merge. This rivalry and its possibilities for growth in this still-lively segment of Broadway and off-Broadway productions is the subject of an article in Friday's New York Times.

Writing in the Times, Joseph Berger reports:

So far, there has been one powwow between Zalmen Mlotek and David Mandelbaum, the artistic directors of

Folksbiene and New Yiddish Rep, respectively. At that amicable meeting last month, the two traded ideas about promoting each other's fare and Folksbiene was asked to consider financing New Yiddish Repertory as an offshoot.

Such amity is no small thing. The narrowing world of Yiddish theater has been bedeviled with one "broyges" — a cherished term for a falling out — after another.

"In a shrinking, small world, there is such hostility between people, and that has to change if anyone has any hope of doing something," said Mr. Mandelbaum.

And that world is certainly shrinking. In 2006, the nation had 152,515 Yiddish speakers, a 15 percent decline from 2000. Although most live in the New York area, many are either over 65 or are Hasidim, who rarely attend theater.

Mr. Wiesenfeld, however, thinks that statistics about Yiddish speakers may be irrelevant. Folksbiene claims to be appealing more and more to non-Yiddish speakers, by staging free performances at colleges and by using English and Russian supertitles projected over the stage.

Mr. Mlotek added that 10 of the last 13 major productions have been original shows, not revivals, and include fare like a Yiddish adaptation of "The Pirates of Penzance" and an offbeat adaptation of a Yiddish story that features images projected onto prayer shawls.

Here is an interview with cast members of "Di Yam Gazlonim" which translates roughly to "The Sea Thieves" followed by a video of an actual performance of its most famous song, "*I Am the Very Model of a Modern Major General*", in Yiddish of course.

Type the URLs in the browser bar to see the videos: http://youtu.be/-YgC8gJLhCA http://youtu.be/ya-KczcuCl0

Shlemiel the First, a Klezmer Musical Comedy, Called Better Than Any Broadway Show

"Better by far than anything currently on Broadway." That's what John Lahr, senior theater critic at The New Yorker magazine, and son of legendary actor Bert Lahr, has to say about *Shlemiel the First*.

Shlemiel the First is an award-winning klezmer musical comedy based on a play of the same name by Isaac Bashevis Singer, about a holy fool sent on an ill-conceived errand that subsequently transforms the inhabitants of Chelm, his impoverished village. It features a live band, on-stage costume changes, and cross-dressing necessitated by the fact that many of the actors play multiple roles (some of the men even play their own wives).

Here's John Lahr's review from the December 12 issue of "The New Yorker."

All fans of the American musical who are sick of boulevard nihilism, movie retreads, choreographic cliché, dopey lyrics, and banal librettos, your ship has come in: "*Shlemiel the First*," the terrific 1994 klezmer musical, adapted by Robert Brustein from Isaac Bashevis Singer's, is being revived, Dec. 13-31, at the Skirball.

David Gordon's elegant production, set in the surreal shtetl landscape of Chelm, jolts an audience out of the habitual.

Shlemiel, its eponymous beadle hero (Michael Iannucci), is a "crazy fool," according to his wife (Amy Warren). He is called upon to spread the wisdom of Gronam Ox, the wisest man of the village council of sages, who earned the laurel by solving a sour-cream shortage. The musical (with splendid lyric by Arnold Weinstein, and music by Hankus Netsky) is a wacky, inspired recounting of his hapless missionary journey. In its artfulness and eloquence, *Shlemiel the First* is better by far than anything currently on Broadway. It returns the musical to its playful, populist roots. Miss it at your peril.

Shlemiel has been significantly reworked since it was originally co-produced by the American Repertory Theater in 1994. This current production comes courtesy of a collaboration between NYU Skirball, The National Yiddish Theatre-Folksbiene, Theatre for a New Audience, or TFANA and Peak Performances at Montclair.

During the last week of rehearsals at The New 42nd Street Studios, a video was made of the Shlemiel cast and crew. In it, they describe their specific roles within the overall production. The individuals featured are (in order of appearance): Kristine Zbornik, Amy Warren, Jeff Brooks, Michael Iannucci, Aaron Netsky, Stephen Cain and Michael Larsen.

So watch the video and watch for revivals of this musical.

Type the URL in your browser address bar to see the video: http://youtu.be/Zre80M62fjE

Yiddish Theater is Alive and Well on Second Avenue (in Montreal)

Yiddish Theater is seeing a revival of sorts, with productions popping up in various locations.

Last year we attended a Folksbiene Theater production of *Shlemiel the First* at the Skirball Center in New York City. Now a new musical production by the Dora Wasserman Yiddish Theater called *On Second Avenue* has opened at the Segal Center for the Performing Arts in Montreal. The show pays tribute to the Yiddish Theater.

Here are two videos about the show. The first has two excerpts from *On Second Avenue*. The second video is a look behind the scenes narrated by the director, musical director, and some of the actors. As one of the actors says, "You can't go to the movies, you can't put on your satellite TV and see this. You've got to get off the couch, get into the car, come here and put your tuches in the seat and witness something live. What you're seeing is unique.

Type the URLs in your browser bar to see the videos:
http://youtu.be/06VLtuc-PwM

http://youtu.be/f7Wj08XkaPo

Fyvush Finkel Celebrates His Career at Folksbiene Theater

In 2010, when he was 88 years old, Fyvush Finkel starred in a show at the Folksbiene Theater in New York highlighting his incredible career, spanning English and Yiddish roles from Second Avenue to modern-day television stardom.

The show was a musical celebration of a life on stage, starring Finkel and his sons Ian Finkel and Elliot Finkel.

Filled with songs, stories, jokes and ample evidence of Finkel's undiminished mastery of show business razzle dazzle, " Fyvush Finkel Live!" brings us this close to one of the last living links to the Yiddish theatre's rich heyday on Second Avenue. But it also introduces us to one of a very select group of actors who are active and successful in both the Yiddish and mainstream worlds. Very few indeed have straddled the traditions of Second Avenue and mainstream entertainment as convincingly as Finkel, "the face that launched a thousand shticks."

Born in Brooklyn, Finkel began his career in the Yiddish theatre as a teenager. After a long stint touring in "Fiddler on the Roof," he starred in the Off-Broadway hit *Little Shop of Horrors* for five years, earned an OBIE in *Café Crown* (which moved to Broadway), and teamed up with his sons Ian and Elliot, and grandson Abbot in two musical revues -- *Finkel's Follies* and *From Second Avenue to Broadway.*

A beloved television star, Finkel earned an Emmy Award in 1994 for *Picket Fences* and he starred in the acclaimed series *Boston Public*, which ran from 2000 to 2004. His most recent appearance was in the opening sequence of the Coen brothers' film *A Serious Man*, in a Yiddish-language dramatization of an erzatz folk tale about a *tzaddik* who may or may not be a dybbuk.

Here's a video clip of Finkel singing a Yiddish classic, *I Am a Boarder By My Wife*.

Type the URL in your browser address bar to see the video: http://youtu.be/GdlCqt38zXE

Tough Guy Actor James Cagney Spoke Yiddish Fluently

James Cagney, the American actor best known for playing tough guys in gangster films and for winning an Oscar for playing George M. Cohan in *Yankee Doodle Dandy*, was a fluent Yiddish speaker.

He spoke Yiddish in a few of his films, including *Taxi* (1932) and *The Fighting 69th* (1940).

As John Farr wrote in The Huffington Post,

About a month ago, I was watching an early Cagney entry called **Taxi!** (1932), and in one early scene, witnessed the diminutive actor of Irish/Norwegian stock speaking Yiddish... not one or two words, mind you, but paragraphs.

And I thought to myself -- yet another reason to love Jimmy Cagney.

As if we needed any more.

In fact, Cagney learned that language fluently growing up dirt-poor on New York's Lower East Side in the early days of the twentieth century. But he had much more than language skills in his favor.

Though compact, he was scrappy and a natural fighter, often protecting his brother from neighborhood bullies. He eventually learned how to box, and became skillful enough to consider doing it for a living.

He also knew how to hustle and sell. He was in constant motion. From early days, he worked several jobs to support his family. Even once he'd made it in Hollywood, he sent his mother the majority of his earnings till the day she died.

Of course Cagney never mentioned that.

Here's the clip of Cagney as a taxi driver in *Taxi.* He watches as a man tries to ask an Irish policeman how to get to Ellis Island to see his wife. When he sees that the man can't get through to the cop and says he has a goyishe kop, Cagney asks the man in Yiddish where he wants to go. The man, surprised, asks Cagney if he is Jewish. Cagney replies, "What then, a shaygetz?

Type the URL in your browser address bar to see the video: http://youtu.be/ynpOEcPdjdk

"Sholem Aleichem: Laughing in the Darkness" Brings Shtetl to Life

Sholem Aleichem, the Yiddish writer and humorist whose vivid portrayals of life in the Eastern European shtetl were the basis for the musical *Fiddler on the Roof* is the subject of a new movie that played a limited engagement in New York City and nearby suburbs.

The film, *Sholem Aleichem: Laughing in the Darkness,* is more than a documentary about the writer's life. It's also a rich portrayal of the history of Eastern European Jewry through his life and work.

Using rarely seen photographs and archive footage, the voices of actors Peter Riegert and Rachel Dratch, and interviews with leading experts and the author's own granddaughter, author Bel Kaufman, the film brings to life as never before Sholem Aleichem's world and his timeless stories.

In his New York Times review titled *So, Would it Hurt You to Go See a Documentary About a Yiddish Writer?,* Stephen Holden wrote:

The movie reveals that Sholem Aleichem was every bit as colorful a figure as the characters in his stories. He was one of 12 children whom his recently widowed father hid with relatives before remarrying, then introduced one by one to the dismay of his shrewish second wife. One of his earliest works was a glossary of his stepmother's curses. As a young man Sholem Aleichem, who was something of a dandy, took a job tutoring the daughter of a wealthy Jewish landowner. When a relationship between them was discovered, he was fired, and the lovers eloped. He was eventually accepted by her family.

Hebrew was the written Jewish language, and Yiddish, a mixture of German, Hebrew and Slavic languages, had no literature, no newspapers or publications. According to the movie, Sholem Aleichem, who founded a Yiddish literary journal, aspired to be "the designer of modern Yiddish literature." This rich, highly expressive language, which one scholar in the film likens to Shakespeare's English, is remembered as having been "a protective shield" and "a portable homeland" separating insular rural Jews from their Russian neighbors.

Sholem Aleichem was a workaholic who, clad in an old bathrobe, would rise at 5 a.m. and write constantly, usually standing up. For more than 25 years he turned out a story a week. Oddly, because Russian was spoken in his home, his six children never learned to write or to speak Yiddish.

Sholem Aleichem was 47 when he came to the United States for the first time in 1906, hoping to be a celebrated playwright, and he was deeply crushed when his first two plays, which opened on the same night, were savaged by critics. He returned to Europe, where he supported himself by giving readings. (The film includes a short, scratchy recording of one.) When he reluctantly returned to America shortly before his death, he received a much warmer reception. More than 100,000 people, The New York Times reported, lined the streets for his funeral in New York in 1916.

The film is listed by Netflix without a release date.

Type the URL in the browser bar to see a video of the trailer: http://vimeo.com/24049917

Egg Rolls and Egg Creams Festival Unites Jewish and Chinese Communities on New York's Lower East Side

In June 2012 the crowds came out to celebrate the 12th annual Egg Rolls and Egg Creams Festival centered around the Eldridge Street Synagogue and Museum on New York's Lower East Side.

As the Bowery Boogie reported:

On the street, a number of tables were serving up the egg rolls and egg creams, with all proceeds from sales benefiting the Eldridge Street Synagogue. The Pickle Guys and Zaro's Bakery, who were event co-sponsors, also had representation. Not everything was food-oriented, though. There were more child-friendly stations dedicated to face painting, arts and crafts, and yarmulka design. All the while, various traditional groups provided a unique soundtrack.

Inside the synagogue proper, the scene was a bit more bustling. A few tables were squeezed into a tiny area behind the pews. One had a *sofer* (scribe) writing out Hebrew names for people on construction paper. His was the most popular. There was also a place for Chinese paintings, calligraphy, and rather intricate origami.

Museum hands told the story of the ornate structure (est. 1887) and a cantor sang some Hebrew hymns. Assembly Speaker Sheldon Silver was also in attendance, and delivered a speech about his connections to the house of worship: How his brother had his Bar Mitzvah there; how his family was involved in its leadership in the 1930s through the 1950s.

The Jewish Daily Forward (*Der Forverts*) was also there, with Yiddish reporter Shmuel Perlin delivering a running narrative of the event, interspersed with historical observations on the establishment of the two communities, their differences and similarities, and the ways they cooperate to maintain one of New York's most colorful neighborhoods.

Here is his video report, in Yiddish with English subtitles.

Type the URL in your browser address bar to see the video: http://youtu.be/KR-n1memRtc

Cooking in Yiddish

A New Yiddish Cooking Show: Est Gesunterheit!

Look out, Emeril Lagasse and Rachael Ray. You've got competition from Rukhl and Eve. And in Yiddish, no less.

The *Forverts*, the original Yiddish daily newspaper, is embracing new programming and new technology to present a series of cooking shows on YouTube.

The video episodes, running under ten minutes, are being posted under the title "Eat in Good Health," or *Est Gesunterheit*. The hosts are Rukhl Schaechter and Eve Jochnowitz.

Schaechter is a writer for the Forward. Jochnowitz, a Yiddish instructor at the Congress for Jewish Culture, is cooking and foodways teacher at Living Traditions Klezkamp and instructor in Jewish Culinary History at The New School University.

Cooking in Yiddish: Varenikes mit Vanschel (Sour Cherry Dumplings)

In the first show, Schaechter and Jochnowitz talk their way in Yiddish through the preparation of *varenikes mit vanschel*, or sour cherry dumplings. English subtitles translate their folksy patter as they work their way through preparing the dough and the sour cherry sauce, singing Yiddish songs about *varenikes* (no kidding!) as they go.

Type the URL in your browser address bar to see the video: http://youtu.be/LnV9wyjQMI8

Cooking In Yiddish: Drink L'Chayim! Horseradish and Jalapeno Vodka With Nut Cake

The Yiddish cooking ladies are back with a new segment, courtesy of yiddish.forward.com, the Yiddish-language web version of the venerable Yiddish newspaper, *Forverts*.

This time they're cooking up a *L'Chayim* to celebrate their biweekly internet show. How do you cook a *L'Chayim*? By making flavored vodkas infused with (we're not kidding) horseradish and jalapeno peppers. There's also a vanilla infused vodka for anyone who can't take the heat. Top it off with a baked-from-scratch nut cake and you've got what it takes to celebrate. And English subtitles are provided so everyone can follow along.

Type the URL in your browser address bar to see the video: http://youtu.be/IrjAh4OqNXg

The Yiddish Chefs Make Potato Soup and Massage a Cabbage

The Forward's Yiddish-speaking chefs are back, this time preparing a dairy potato soup and red cabbage slaw for your enjoyment.

As usual, Rukhl Schaechter and Eve Jochnowitz carry on a lively conversation, all in Yiddish, while going about their food preparation.

As in previous episodes of their cooking show, Est Gezunterheit, the English subtitles give us a painless lesson in spoken Yiddish, and a few new words to let us show off our language skills by introducing a Yiddish word into our daily conversations. Here is the crop of Yiddish words used in this video.

Potatoes: Kartuffle

Soft: Veich
Putting in: Arain shittin
Dill: Creep
Garlic: Knubble
Cabbage: Kroit
Pour: Geese
Sink: Oopguss
Squeeze: Kvetch
Massage: Massajieren

Type the URL in your browser address bar to see the video: http://youtu.be/hMcDDPrM6iU

Make Your Own Hamantaschen With the Forverts' Yiddish Chefs

When Purim time comes around, it's time to bake your own hamantaschen with Rukhl Schaechter and Eve Jochnowitz, the Yiddish-speaking and bantering chefs of Forverts, the Yiddish (and original) version of the Jewish Daily Forward.

We've posted just about every one of their cooking videos over the last few years, which tend to coincide with the onset of Jewish holidays throughout the year.

In this episode, the Yiddish chefs are wearing Purim costumes as they bake apricot and poppy seed (mohn) hamantaschen from scratch. The 16-minute video includes a short commercial for Cherry Heering and Coffee Heering liqueurs, in which two clown-costumed mixologists conjure up Cherry Seinfeld and Coffee Anan drinks.

We usually pick up a few new Yiddish words from these videos, but maybe we've seen so many of them that most of the Yiddish doesn't seem new. But we did find a good new one: How do you say rolling pin in Yiddish? Volgerholtz!

Type the URL in your browser address bar to see the video: http://youtu.be/B0EttJLP2BE

The Yiddish Chefs Return With Gluten-Free (and Varnish-Free) Kashe Varnishkes

It's time for another cooking demo, and if you listen carefully, a lesson in spoken Yiddish.

Yes, the Forward's *Est Gezunterheit* chefs are back in another video from their cooking series. This time the Yiddish-speaking cooking ladies prepare gluten-free *kashe varnishkes* in a video just posted on YouTube.

We like these videos because you get a cooking lesson combined with a Yiddish lesson, just by listening to the light conversation between the chefs and reading the English subtitles.

From this video, we learned some Yiddish words that we didn't know before. Here they are:

Bowties = Schnips
Frying pan = Petelnye
Jagged cutting wheel = Tchabattateh schneidredel
Squeeze = Kneitch

Type the URL in your browser address bar to see the video: http://youtu.be/2po8UMBdCUY

The Yiddish Cooking Ladies Go Vegetarian: Rice Dumplings with Mushrooms

This time the Yiddish-speaking cooking ladies venture into vegetarian territory.

Using a cookbook printed in Vilna, Lithuania, in 1938, Rukhl Schaechter and Eve Yochnowitz take us through the steps to prepare rice kneidlach (dumplings) filled with mushrooms and onions and served in a mushroom sauce.

We like these videos because you get a cooking lesson combined with a Yiddish lesson, just by listening to the light conversation between the chefs and reading the English subtitles.

From this session, we learned some Yiddish words that we didn't know before. Here they are:

Mushrooms = Shvemlach

Frying = Pregelen

Broth = Yoich

Onions = Tzibelach (we knew this one already, from the old Yiddish curse, *"Zolst vaksen vi a tsibeleh mit'n kop in dr'erd - You should grow like an onion with your head in the ground"*).

Parsley = Petrushke

Dill = Krip

Rice = Rice

Sauce = Sauce

Type the URL in your browser address bar to see the video: http://youtu.be/pVQF3Mfgrno

It's the Yiddish Cooking Ladies Again With Apple Kugel and Vegetarian Chopped Liver

If you've been a regular reader of Jewish Humor Central, you're probably familiar with the Yiddish speaking kitchen wizards from the Jewish Forward (Forverts). Since May 2010 we've brought you episodes from their periodic web-based cooking show, Est Gezunterheit (Eat in Good Health).

So what are Rukhl Schaechter and Eve Jochnowitz up to this time? They're making recipes from the files of the late Yiddish actress Shifra Lerer, who has also appeared a few times on Jewish Humor Central. This episode includes Lerer's Austrian Apple Kugel (or as they say, Kigel) and Vegetarian Chopped Liver (Gehakte Leber.)

Watch as the Forward's chefs banter in Yiddish as they chop onions and peel apples. OK, so it's not the Food Network, but it has a unique Yiddishe taam that you won't get from Rachael Ray or Paula Deen. If you watch carefully and read the English titles on the bottom of the screen, you can actually learn some Yiddish. In paying homage to Shifra Lerer, Jochnowitz launches into a bit of tango dancing, with her cell phone as a partner. Try looking for that on the Food Network!

Type the URL in your browser address bar to see the video: http://youtu.be/IbVvwgpZsQk

Latkes mit Punchkes --and It's All in Yiddish

The Forverts Yiddish Chefs are back, just in time for a complete Chanukah party -- Potato Latkes, Pumpkin Donuts, Black Cherry Punch, and Hot Coffee Latte.

We've been sharing these cooking-shmoozing sessions with you as they are posted, and we always learn a few new Yiddish words from Rukhl Schaechter and Eve Jochnowitz as they putter and patter about the kitchen.

What did we learn this time? Donuts are called *sufganiyot* in Hebrew, but did you know they're called *punchkes* in Yiddish? And a food processor? It's a *mish-machine*. Buttermilk? *Maslinkeh*. Nutmeg? *Mushkat*. Pumpkin? *Dinye*.

And that cherry liqueur that they use for the cold drink? Now it's called Heering Cherry Liqueur, but we remember it back in the day (way way back) as Cherry Heering, pronounced by our appetizing-loving relatives as Cherry *Herring* (yes, like the fish,). Who knows, maybe in Denmark where Peter Heering created the drink, it's really pronounced *herring*. But we'll take it with a twist of Yiddish and enjoy it either way with our dinye punchkes.

Type the URL in your browser address bar to see the video: http://youtu.be/jeYTeoaxPm0

The Yiddish Chefs Cook Up a Peasant Meal on the Yiddish Farm

Our favorite Yiddish chefs have journeyed to the Yiddish Farm to use its produce and kitchen to create a peasant meal featuring white beets and spinach, while chatting with each other in Yiddish (with English subtitles, of course.)

Here are some of the Yiddish words used in this video and their English translations:

Goyshen (Goshen)

Berikes (Beets)

Shpinat (Spinach)

Shrotzim (Bugs)

Shrotzimlach (Little Bugs)

Opgossen (Sink)

Grintzen (Veggies)

Skorinkeh (Bread Crust)

Type the URL in your browser address bar to see the video: http://youtu.be/EMquqC5bn8M

The Yiddish Chefs Make Chicken Fricassee and Rice With Apples

The Yiddish-speaking chefs from the *Forverts*, the Yiddish-language version of The Jewish Daily Forward, are back with a couple of recipes that could make it easy to prepare a pre-Yom Kippur fast meal or one of the meals for the week-long holiday of Sukkot.

The ladies, Rukhl Schaechter and Eve Jochnowitz, chatter and make small talk in Yiddish while preparing Chicken Fricassee and a vegetarian dish of rice with apples.

We've run most of their cooking episodes since they started the series in May 2010.

One of the kicks we get out of the series is the painless Yiddish lesson that comes from listening to their banter as the English translation appears in subtitles. For example, *gehakte knobbel* has much more character than minced garlic, and *hoit* is much more expressive than chicken skin.

The recipes in this series, including this one, are not what you'd find in a fancy fusion restaurant, but they do offer a look back at the life of Jews in Eastern Europe.

Type the URL in your browser address bar to see the video: http://youtu.be/n7-lkvm1XW8

The Yiddish Chefs Are Back With a Chicken Dinner for Simchat Torah

Once again Rukhl Schaechter and Eve Yochnowitz, the Forward's Yiddish chefs, are back with a pair of recipes that may be just right for the last two days (one day in Israel) of the Sukkot holiday, Shemini Atzeret and Simchat Torah. Or you can make them for a Shabbat meal or any other occasion.

These dishes are a traditional French-style roast chicken and a Sephardic rice pilaf with noodles, all easy to prepare as shown in the video. We even get a few bonuses -- a Yiddish commercial for Empire's microwaveable ready to roast garlic and herb chicken, and some lively klezmer music in the background.

As always with these segments of "Est Gezunterheit" we get a few new juicy Yiddish words to add to our vocabulary. The words from this episode are:

Small chicken: Hindel (although the chefs joke that "tshikn" sounds like a Yiddish word)
Roast chicken: Gebrutene hin
Side dish: By-gericht
Rinsing: Oopvashen, or shvenken
Kitchen shears: Koch sher
Plastic: Plastic
Stuffing the chicken: Oonshtuppen dos hindle

Vegetable spray: Shpritz boimel
Piercing: Oonshtechen

Type the URL in your browser address bar to see the video: http://youtu.be/CgbdH2h2Fxc

Look Out, Rachael And Emeril -- Here Comes "Feed Me Bubbe"

In 2008, an 83-year-old short, stooped, white-haired Massachusetts grandmother with a kindly face was happily retired from her bank job. Then her grandson Avrom Honig graduated from Worcester State College with a degree in communications. That was the start of a new career for both of them -- Avrom as the producer and Bubbe (she will not disclose her real name) as the star of an online cooking show.

Now, 30 episodes later, as Linda Matchan wrote in the Boston Globe,

...she's inundated with e-mail — "without exaggeration, hundreds, even thousands" — from fans from as far away as China and Africa who want help roasting chicken or stuffing cabbage, or to confide in her about their *tsuris* (troubles).

She's got a website (http://www.feedmebubbe.com), a frequently updated Facebook page ("on the set right now working on the *cholent* episode"), and an online store selling her T-shirts, aprons, even a "Feed Me Bubbe" ringtone (original klezmer music, composed by a fan).

Bubbe's newfound fame is a uniquely 21st century phenomenon, made possible in a world where anyone who blogs, tweets, Facebooks, or YouTubes can vault to celebrity. But this is also what makes Bubbe's story so unusual. Until recently, her life was so low-tech that she thought the Internet "came out of the air, just like nothing."

Though she didn't set out to do so, Bubbe has managed to stand out from the pack by embracing the new technology while just being herself, cooking old-fashioned dishes in an old-fashioned kitchen in old-fashioned ways. In the process, she has tapped into a market of peripatetic, family-starved young people who are hungry for more than just chicken soup. They're hungry for Bubbes.

For that very reason, Bubbe - who lives in a suburb west of Boston - doesn't disclose her real name on the show, and she declined to give it to the Globe as well. "I never want to be recognized. People write me and say I remind them of their own grandmother," says Bubbe, who believes she fills a void in the lives of grandmother-less viewers. "So how can I have another name?"

Feed Me Bubbe: Sweet and Sour Meatballs

In the video below, Bubbe congratulates YouTube on its fifth anniversary and notes that *Feed Me Bubbe* is celebrating its fourth anniversary. We follow this with one of Bubbe's cooking videos in which she prepares sweet and sour meatballs.

Type the URLs in your browser bar to see the videos:
http://youtu.be/FR8yWOdB79s
http://youtu.be/0CngRcNJSQ4

Bubbe Is Back Again, This Time With Tzimmes For Simchat Torah

Bubbe of Feedmebubbe.com is back to show you how to make a side dish of tzimmes for the last days of Sukkot and Simchat Torah.

This video of Bubbe is not from her regular series on her website, but from The Food Network's show, In Search of Real Food with Dave Lieberman. So learn a few tips, and laugh with Bubbe as she makes cooking look easy.

Type the URL in your browser address bar to see the video: http://youtu.be/a42v3qp6-jU

"Feed Me Bubbe" Grandmother Makes Passover Apple Matzah Kugel

Bubbe is back, to share a video of her preparing and baking recipe number 36, Apple Matzah Kugel. The recipe also appears on page 171 of her book, Feed Me Bubbe, which is available in paperback and Kindle editions.

Type the URL in your browser address bar to see the video: http://youtu.be/AUkfSVNyZi8

Gefilte Fish From Scratch...And In Yiddish

Just a few pages back we posted a story titled "Look Out, Rachael and Emeril -- Here Comes "Feed Me, Bubbe." The story was about a grandmother in Massachusetts, known only as Bubbe, who is the star of an online cooking show.

Now the Bubbe of "Feed Me, Bubbe" may have some competition. Earlier this year, Bubby Chanele Gonshor of Montreal visited her granddaughter, Frayda Gonshor Cohen of Berkeley, California, and showed her how to prepare gefilte fish from scratch -- from buying the fish in a store to serving it.

In this video, Bubby Chanele shows every step along the way, narrating in Yiddish, while English subtitles make it easy to follow even for anyone who doesn't understand the *mamaloshen* (mother tongue).

We don't know if, after watching it, you're motivated to try the day-long process yourself, or to take one of the easy ways out, like buying gefilte fish off the supermarket shelf in jars, from take-out stores, or in pre-shaped frozen loaves to finish cooking at home. But either way, you're bound to have a renewed appreciation for the loving efforts of countless grandmas, bubbes, and bubbys who have prepared this traditional dish for generations of children and grandchildren.

Type the URL in your browser address bar to see the video: http://youtu.be/Z_q2pyW_tTo

Cooking With the Bubbe: Potato Latkes for Hanukkah

Some of our most popular blog posts have been of grandmothers, or bubbes, cooking Jewish foods using their own recipes.

First we shared a recipe for sweet and sour meatballs by a bubbe from Worcester, Massachusetts. Then we shared a recipe for gefilte fish, watching a bubby from Montreal buying the the fish in the store and all the steps along the way to serving it on the table.

Now we think it's time to stock up on the essentials for making *heimishe* potato latkes from scratch.

Who ever thought the internet would awaken the star potential of bubbes everywhere who are probably saying "Food Network, Shmood Network. Why don't you show me in my kitchen?"

So here is "The Bubbe" showing us how to prepare homemade potato (and also veggie) latkes. Who is the Bubbe? She's Lisa Murik from Silver Spring, Maryland -- an octogenarian, holocaust survivor, and great-grandmother who is much beloved by family, friends, and the greater community for spreading her love of food.

You can read her story at www.thebubbe.com. Then, it's time to start cooking.

Type the URL in your browser address bar to see the video: http://youtu.be/IDSn7kae0FQ

A Note from the Author

IF YOU ENJOYED THIS BOOK, YOU CAN GET ALL SEVEN
INDIVIDUAL VOLUMES AND THE COMPLETE COLLECTION
IN A SINGLE VOLUME

AT AMAZON.COM

I hope you enjoyed reading the anecdotes in this book and watching the videos that they link to. This book is the fifth in a series that organizes and elaborates on the hundreds of blog posts that have appeared on the blog Jewish Humor Central over the last three years. Unlike the blog, which presents a joke or anecdote from a random category each day, these volumes are organized by major and minor category to make it easy for you to find all of the items relating to a category.

I am available for presentation of this material to your synagogue, JCC, or other organization in the form of lectures on Jewish humor that survey the broad range of topics in these books or focus on the individual categories.

If you would like more information about these lectures, please contact me at akustan@gmail.com.

Al Kustanowitz

CPSIA information can be obtained
at www.ICGtesting.com
Printed in the USA
FSHW01n0716220618
49699FS